Self-Esteem for Men

5 Simple But Overlooked Methods to Start an Inner Journey and Which Will Stop You Being a Doormat

By

John Adams

© Copyright 2018 - All rights reserved.

The content contained within this book may not be reproduced, duplicated or transmitted without direct written permission from the author or the publisher.

Under no circumstances will any blame or legal responsibility be held against the publisher, or author, for any damages, reparation, or monetary loss due to the information contained within this book. Either directly or indirectly.

Legal Notice:

This book is copyright protected. This book is only for personal use. You cannot amend, distribute, sell, use, quote or paraphrase any part, or the content within this book, without the consent of the author or publisher.

Disclaimer Notice:

Please note the information contained within this document is for educational and entertainment purposes only. All effort has been executed to present accurate, up to date, and reliable, complete information. No warranties of any kind are declared or implied. Readers acknowledge that the author is not engaging in the rendering of legal, financial, medical or professional advice. The content within this book has been derived from various sources. Please consult a licensed professional before attempting any techniques outlined in this book.

By reading this document, the reader agrees that under no circumstances is the author responsible for any losses, direct or indirect, which are incurred as a result of the use of information contained within this document, including, but not limited to, — errors, omissions, or inaccuracies.

Table of Contents

Chapter 1: Introduction: What Is Self-Esteem?   7
    Is Self-Esteem an Inherent Trait?   8
    Loss of Self-Esteem   9
    Importance of Self-Esteem   10

Chapter 2: The Components of Building Self-Esteem   15
    The Practice of Living Consciously   16
    The Practice of Self-Acceptance   18
    The Practice of Self-Responsibility   19
    The Practice of Self-Assertiveness   21
    The Practice of Living with Purpose   23
    The Practice of Personal Integrity   25

Chapter 3: Habits and How to Use Them for Good   31
    The Cue   32
    The Routine   36
    The Reward   36

Chapter 4: Practical Examples   41
    The Practice of Living Consciously   41
    The Practice of Self-Acceptance   45
    The Practice of Self-Responsibility   48
    The Practice of Self-Assertiveness   52
    The Practice of Living Purposefully   55

The Practice of Personal Integrity	58
Chapter 5: Workbook	**61**
Conclusion	**73**

Chapter 1: Introduction: What Is Self-Esteem?

Self-esteem reflects a person's sense of self-worth or self-respect. 'Do you consider yourself a worthy man?' is the question you need to answer to get a basic understanding of your current level of self-esteem. It is a trait that reflects your own opinion about yourself. Other self-beliefs that have a direct effect on the level of self-esteem include:

- Do you think the job you do aligns with your capabilities and qualifications?
- Do you think other people respect you and your profession?
- Do you think your salary and remuneration matches the work you do?
- Do you think your family and friends appreciate you for what you are?
- Do you think your children are proud of having you as their father?
- Do you think you are a good-looking man?
- Do you think you have great social skills?
- Do you believe that you have a good standing in your community and social circle?

Psychologists refer to self-esteem as a personality trait that describes an overall sense of personal value. Therefore, self-esteem can be defined as a measure of how you value and estimate your worth. Unlike other personality traits, such as confidence, which can differ depending on the situation and circumstance, self-esteem tends to endure for a person across all aspects of his life. So, if you have a low level of self-esteem in your personal life, then you probably have similar levels in your professional life as well.

Is Self-Esteem an Inherent Trait?

Typically, self-esteem is an acquired trait that people can learn and master if they put their mind to it. However, genetic factors could play a small role in a person's aptitude for self-esteem. So, if someone has an inherent tendency to be proud of himself, then this person will find it easier to build and develop his self-esteem than someone who is genetically predisposed to be uncertain of himself.

However, it is an irrefutable truth that biology need not define your destiny. You have control over how you want to be and what desires you want to achieve. With a bit of patience, hard work, and commitment, it is possible to build and develop your self-esteem to high levels. Consequently, your ability to succeed in life will also go up a few notches. Here are some examples of strong and powerful men who managed to overcome the overwhelming challenges of low self-esteem:

John Lennon – As a young adult, this British music star and co-founder of The Beatles believed that part of him was a loser and the other part of him believed himself to be God Almighty.

These conflicting emotions are typical of a man with low self-esteem. He failed in nearly all his tests and exams right through his school and college. He worked hard at building his strengths which, in turn, helped him build and develop his self-esteem to become the music superstar that he became.

Thomas Edison – Yes, absolutely! That famous scientist who is one of the few men with the highest number of patents in his name struggled with low self-esteem. He was physically weak and suffered from multiple health issues. He became deaf as a child. You can only begin to imagine the pain and agony he must have gone through before he rose to superstardom in the world of science.

Therefore, if you are a victim of low self-esteem, you need not fret. There are many ways in which you can raise your self-esteem to align it with your true worth.

Loss of Self-Esteem

If self-esteem is not an inherent trait, then it means it is constructed in our minds through our interactions with the outside world. So, what are the factors that deplete our self-esteem? Many of the factors that affect our self-esteem typically begin in our childhood. Here are some of them:

Constantly disapproving parents and teachers – If the elders always found fault with you and focused on what you didn't do well, your self-esteem is bound to be negatively impacted

Uninvolved parents – The feeling of neglect you face if your parents were excessively busy with their lives and did not have the time and energy to nurture you is a primary reason for low self-esteem.

Conflict among parents - If your parents were always bickering and fighting with each other, your confusion about whose side to take is bound to lead to low self-esteem.

Importance of Self-Esteem

Why is self-esteem important for everyone? Mark Twain said, "No man can be comfortable without his own approval." Oscar Wilde said, "To love yourself is the start of a lifelong romance that never loses its appeal." The value and importance of self-esteem cannot be undermined. Here are some excellent reasons why you must begin to work on your self-esteem right away:

- Self-esteem is one of the primary differences between success and failure, both in your personal and professional life
- Self-esteem drives your outlook on life; high self-esteem gives you a positive outlook and low self-esteem results in a negative outlook.
- Self-esteem directly impacts your self-confidence and assertiveness; when you are certain of your worth, your self-confidence and assertiveness will shine through.

- Self-esteem is something that gets reflected in your physical profile; a man with low self-esteem will hold his head high, and a man with low self-esteem will have his head hanging in shame or guilt or both
- Self-esteem is the starting point to build respect and dignity in your world
- Self-esteem directly impacts your happiness

Signs of Healthy Self-Esteem:

- The ability to say no firmly
- Confidence
- A positive outlook on life
- Ability to identify and accept both strengths and weaknesses
- Ability to articulate needs clearly and strongly
- Ability to accept criticism positively

Signs of Low Self-Esteem:

- Lack of confidence
- A negative outlook on life
- Inability to articulate needs and desires
- Feelings of anxiety, shame, depression, etc.
- Inability to accept criticism in the right spirit
- A strong belief of being useless and worthless
- Fear of failure

Quiz to Discover Your Current Level of Self-Esteem

Answer these questions honestly, which will help you assess your current level of self-esteem. Once you know which areas need to be addressed, you can work on improving them:

Q1. It is very easy for me to feel hurt

1. Most of the time   2. Sometimes   3. Almost never

Q2. Even if I know and believe that someone is giving me constructive criticism, I get hurt and angry.

1. Most of the time   2. Sometimes   3. Almost never

Q3. I get angry with myself even if I make an understandable and acceptable mistake

1. Most of the time   2. Sometimes   3. Almost never

Q4. I ask other people about the decisions I must take instead of making my own decisions

1. Most of the time   2. Sometimes   3. Almost never

Q5. I always accept my team's decision even if I don't agree with them

1. Most of the time   2. Sometimes   3. Almost never

Q6. I am uncomfortable receiving praise and compliments

1. Most of the time   2. Sometimes   3. Almost never

Q7. I don't feel good enough often, and I feel 'I don't really measure up' to my peers.

1. Most of the time   2. Sometimes   3.   Almost never

Q8. I engage in negative self-talk, often telling myself things like, "I don't deserve that promotion in the office," or "I can never complete the report on time."

1. Most of the time   2. Sometimes   3.   Almost never

Q9. When I see myself in the mirror, I tell myself, "How ugly I am!"

1. Most of the time   2. Sometimes   3.   Almost never

Q10. I find myself saying sorry frequently, even if the mistake is not mine.

1. Most of the time   2. Sometimes   3.   Almost never

Analyzing your self-discovery quiz - If most of the answers to the above questions are 'almost never,' then your self-esteem level is healthy. Everyone feels uncertain and angry at some point in their life, especially if they don't like what they see. As long as these negative experiences don't happen often, your self-esteem is quite healthy.

If most of your answers were 'sometimes,' then you could be at risk of entering low self-esteem levels, although you may not really be suffering from psychological problems like depression. However, you do tend to have a pessimistic view of yourself, and life in general, which is not a good sign. It might be wise to buckle up and get your self-esteem up. It might even be a good idea to seek professional help.

If most of your answers were 'almost never,' then this is a real cause for concern, and it makes sense to approach a professional and seek help immediately before things reach irreversible levels.

Chapter 2: The Components of Building Self-Esteem

Men need a healthy dose of self-esteem to achieve their best potential in their personal and professional lives. Healthy self-esteem will help you do exceedingly well in your profession, earn well-deserving accolades, and get promotions, and consequently lots more money.

At home too, a healthy dose of self-esteem will make your loved ones feel proud of you. They will love and adore you for who you are without feeling bad about your shortcomings because you have chosen to accept your weaknesses with humility and an approach to improve yourself.

Nathanial Branden is known as one of the most famous and influential writers about self-esteem and its importance for success and happiness. His most famous book is called *The Six Pillars of Self-Esteem,* in which he extols the six components that make up this critical personality trait. The six components of self-esteem include:

1. Conscious living
2. Self-acceptance
3. Self-responsibility
4. Self-assertiveness
5. Living with purpose
6. Personal integrity

Knowing and understanding each of the six components will help you develop your self-esteem wholesomely.

The Practice of Living Consciously

Most of us are drifting along our life paths, simply accepting what comes our way, and then finding reasons for resentment and unhappiness. For example, you get up each morning, brush, wash, dress, have breakfast, and commute to work Are you conscious of the sensations and feelings associated with these routine activities? Do you recall the experience of brushing your teeth or having a bath? Do you recall the taste, texture, and color of the dish you had during breakfast? Do you recall hugging your wife and children with happiness and joy?

Most of us don't even consider these routine activities as important, let alone trying to do them consciously. Living consciously means being in the moment at all times. Living consciously means you are immersed in and engaged with your life knowing and feeling your desires and purposes. Living consciously means focusing all your energies deliberately and purposefully towards achieving your dreams and desires. Here are some great tips to live consciously:

Embrace your true self; warts and all – Don't try to lie to yourself about the kind of person you are. If you are great at managing people, accept this quality with pride, not arrogance. If you have a problem controlling your finances, then accept this quality with humility and without rancor.

Be aware of how you spend your time and energy – Focus on your thoughts and where your attention is going. When you are working on a report at your office, is your entire attention on that task or is your mind wandering to the office party that took place last week even as your hand moves mechanically over the keyboard typing out the important report?

When you are in a project meeting, is your undivided attention in the meeting or has your mind wandered to your child's school report card? When you are doing a task, be conscious of whether that task is contributing to your success, or is it something that is quite irrelevant to it? This focused approach to each element in your life will ensure you don't waste these two precious and depleting resources: time and energy.

Build self-awareness – What are the priorities in your life? Is it your career, your family, health, love of travel and adventure, making money, or anything else? This increased self-awareness will help you understand whether your activities and way of life are aligned with your life purposes or not.

The Practice of Self-Acceptance

Self-acceptance means accepting yourself the way you are without being judgmental. For example, you are great at people management and everyone in your family and office come to you to solve conflicts. However, you fall short when it comes to computer skills. Simply accept both these qualities without liking or disliking them.

Self-acceptance is a trait that allows you to be who you are without the need for external approval. When you accept yourself, you are merely being okay with who you are at that point in time. It does not mean you are unwilling to change and work on your weaknesses.

Accepting yourself, warts and all, only means you are at a particular point right now, and you are fine with it and have no regrets about being there. However, self-acceptance does not mean you are going to remain there. In fact, self-acceptance is the first step to making positive changes for self-improvement. Here are a few tips to help you achieve self-acceptance:

List your negative aspects and let them go – This approach will help you look at your weaknesses without judgment even as you let go of them. Forgive and show compassion to yourself as you let the judgmental attitudes about your weaknesses go.

Acknowledge your feelings – For example, if your boss said something hurtful to you, then accept the feeling of being hurt. You don't have to react to the feeling. But you should also not suppress the emotion. Don't think about who is wrong or right. Merely accept the pain of the emotion.

Don't be scared of failure – Make failure your ally, because nothing is a better teacher than failure. Failures contribute significantly to our lowered self-esteem. If you accept failure as an opportunity instead of a shaming act, then your self-esteem will not be hit badly.

The Practice of Self-Responsibility

You have learned to live consciously and to accept yourself the way you are. Now, it is time to take responsibility to make positive changes for yourself. Self-responsibility is an attribute given to people who don't view themselves as victims of external circumstances. Instead, they learn to take responsibility and act in a manner that will bring about positive changes in their lives.

For example, if you are poor at computer skills, you cannot blame the computer world for that, can you? Or, for that matter, you cannot play the victim card and say that no one is teaching you. That is a sure sign of low self-esteem. It is up to you to enroll in a computer class or find an online course that you can do at your convenience or find any other resource to build your skills.

The more you learn on your own, the better you get at that skill. People who refuse to help you are actually doing you a favor by increasing your self-reliance. By facing a situation in which you have to learn a skill to survive, you will be driven to learn it in the most effective way possible, ensuring you are on top of the game.

Self-responsibility also includes taking responsibility for your happiness. If you say that the dinner your wife cooked was bad and that made you unhappy, then that is playing the victim card. An alternate solution would be perhaps to order dinner or better still, cook yourself. It is highly likely that your wife will learn from you and improve her cooking skills.

Self-responsibility begins with the awareness that you can take control of your life. There should be no one else but you who is on the driver's seat of your life. It also includes the awareness of the elements in your life that you have no control over.

For example, you are late for work already, and the bus also arrives late. The control to be on time to work is in your hands. However, the control of making the bus come on time is really not in your hands. In such a scenario, you must include the factor of the late-coming of the bus as part of your control by leaving early from home to catch an earlier commute.

As you learn to live consciously, you will become increasingly aware of elements that are under your control and those that are not under your control. Some tips to take on self-responsibility:

- Accept that you are responsible for your thoughts, words, feelings, responses, and everything your body and mind are involved in. Your thoughts are coming from your mind, words from your mouth, feelings from your heart and mind, and so forth. No one can make you do, think, or say something unless you choose to do, think or say.
- Stop blaming and complaining about everyone around you including yourself. Blaming is the ultimate weapon of a victim. It also robs you of the power to change the situation for the better.
- Avoid taking issues personally. The world does not revolve around you. This attitude will help you take disagreements in your stride without feeling as if you are being personally attacked

The Practice of Self-Assertiveness

The practice of self-assertiveness comes when you live your life by your values and principles, by honoring your needs and desires to achieve your personal goals and life purposes. So, you start your journey of building self-esteem by first learning to live consciously, then accepting yourself as who you are, followed by taking responsibility for what is happening in your life and your happiness. The next component of self-esteem is to identify, honor, and assert your needs and desires.

Self-assertiveness is also referred to as authenticity which means you are projecting your true inner self to the outside world. Additionally, self-assertiveness includes your ability to articulate your needs and desires to the world when the need arises.

For example, if honesty is a crucial value in your life, then speaking, behaving, and standing for honesty should be your primary focus even in the face of rising unpopularity for your actions. Fear of aversion should not drive you away from your life's values and principles.

Therefore, living with self-assertiveness is, perhaps, one of the most difficult self-esteem components to achieve. Living consciously will make you realize that it is far easier to give in to popular demands (against your values and principles) than to be self-assertive.

For example, a big promotion is coming up and you don't want to displease your boss. He repeatedly calls you into work on weekends. You have promised to take your kids on a family picnic one weekend after letting your boss know that you will not come into work. He agrees, but again on Friday, he demands that you come to work the next day.

Do you stand by your promise to your kids or do you break the promise to please your boss and increase your chances of getting that coveted promotion? These dilemmas will keep raising their ugly heads in your life and challenging your self-assertiveness. Your ability to withstand the challenges and come out unscathed is what will define your level of self-esteem.

The Practice of Living with Purpose

When you have a purpose in life, you don't merely exist. A definitive reason behind the 'why' of your life drives you to use your passion and talents to thrive in a happy and meaningful life. Winston Churchill said, *"It is not enough to have simply lived. We should be determined to live for something."*

A purpose in your life gives you determination and focus to stay on your goal path. This forward march towards a set goal is a huge contributor to self-esteem. As you progress on your journey and measure the progress and see how close you are getting to your goal, you will raise your self-esteem a few notches.

If you are a man who is struggling to find purpose in life, don't fret. You are one amongst millions of other men going through a similar situation. That you have woken up to the fact that you lack a purpose is the first step to finding your purpose. The earlier you work on your life purpose, the easier it will be for you to get a direction in life.

Each of us has different purposes and you should not be compelled to follow anyone else's path except your own. There are no right and wrong purposes in life too. *"People take different paths for happiness and fulfillment. Just because they are not on your path does not mean they have got lost,"* says the Dalai Lama.

Therefore, it is imperative that you find your purpose for yourself. While you can take the advice and suggestions of well-wishers, the ultimate decision should be yours and yours alone. Take self-responsibility for your life purpose. Here are some tips to find your life purpose:

Identify your strengths – Make a list of things you are reasonably good at and a list of things in which you are exceptional. In fact, you could be so good at some things that you wonder why others find it difficult to do. It could be anything including an amazing ability to read people, to merely glance at balance sheets and find mistakes, a skill at being extremely detailed, a great communicator, or anything else.

Identify your passion – What do you care deeply about? Nelson Mandela said, *"There is no passion in living small; in choosing a life that is less than what you are capable of."* You don't have to have a fire in your belly to find your passion or live a meaningful life of purpose. You don't have to be driven by a deep desire to start an orphanage or old-age home. Of course, if you have this desire, go right ahead and do it.

However, on a practical level, identify what triggers your emotions, what lights you up, and what gives you a sense of peace. If you still have problems with finding your passion, simply start by writing down who and what you care about. What is closest to your heart? And move forward from there.

Find out where and in what you add the most value — Identifying what you serve best is the final step to finding your purpose. Ask yourself these questions:

- What kind of problems are you great at solving?
- What kinds of needs of other people can you easily meet?
- Who are the people you are best placed to serve?
- What kind of struggles can you help ease in other people?
- Where is the place you continuously add value?

The ideas that are at the junction of the above three points will give you a direction to your life purpose.

The Practice of Personal Integrity

Now that five of the six components of self-esteem are covered, you are well on your way to building healthy levels of self-esteem. The final and, perhaps, the largest contributor to self-esteem is personal integrity. Personal integrity reflects your ability to lead a life that is aligned with your values and principles. Living by your values enhances your self-belief that you are sufficiently equipped to lead your life on your terms and using your skills and strengths.

Take that example of having to stand up to your boss and asserting yourself so that you can keep your promise of taking your children for a weekend picnic. Now, your personal integrity will come into play here. For example, if your life purpose is your career and you are driven by your personal integrity, then you choose to become unpopular with your children and give in to the demands of your boss. Alternately, if your life purpose and value is driven by family and loved ones, then by showcasing your personal integrity, you choose to incur the wrath of your boss by standing your ground and saying you will not come into the office that particular weekend and, perhaps, lower your chances of promotion.

So, there are no right and wrong answers to life's questions. Your actions and behaviors will make some people happy and some people unhappy. The crucial element for personal integrity is to ask yourself if you are reflecting your true self to the outside world or are you pretending to do something simply to please people. The former behavior rates your personal integrity at a high level.

When you choose to reject your personal values and stray from the path of personal integrity, it is quite likely that, for a little while, the people you tried to please are happy with your choice. However, sooner rather than later, you will find this conflicting behavior affecting your life negatively, because not living your life on your terms is equal to rejecting yourself, which is the first step to lowered self-esteem.

So, working on the six components as propounded by Nathaniel Branden gives you the perfect direction to build and develop your self-esteem. Take the following quizzes on the six components to understand your current levels.

Self-Assessment Questionnaire for Living Consciously

The following questions are based on Neuro-Linguistic Programming techniques that help you understand your current level of living consciously. Each of the questions (from Q1-Q6) should be answered with one of the following options:

A. I don't sense anything, and I am not aware
B. Sometimes I do sense, but I don't know how to control them
C. I can sense clearly and vividly

Q1. Do you see the visuals in your mind?

Q2. Do you hear your inner voices clearly?

Q3. Do you connect with your feelings and emotions deeply?

Q4. Do you recognize and identify people, situations, and your own inner thoughts that trigger your reactions?

Q5. Do you know your limitations?

Q6. Do you sense your inner conflicts?

For the next set of 4 questions, write down your answers in detail:

Q7. Have you identified your personal beliefs and values? What are they?

Q8. What is the thing you value the most in your life and why?

Q9. How do the people in your life, including family and loved ones, friends, social circle, and co-workers impact your life?

Q10. What are your strengths and weaknesses?

Self-Assessment Questionnaire for Self-Acceptance

Q1. Are your life goals based on your needs and desires?

Q2. Are you always comparing your capabilities with those of others?

Q3. Are you always trying to grade your work and yourself as good, bad, average, not enough?

Q4. If your work is criticized, do you feel bad about it?

Q5. Are you always thinking about your weaknesses and rarely giving yourself credit for your strengths?

Self-Assessment Questionnaire for Self-Responsibility

Q1. Do you think that your behaviors, reactions, and responses are your own?

Q2. Do you accept responsibility for your behaviors and reactions, even if you know that something outside of you caused them?

Q3. Do you accept responsibility for your physical and mental health?

Q4. Do you accept that only you are responsible for your happiness?

Q5. Do you believe that your values and principles should be your own and not borrowed from other people who influence your life?

Self-Assessment Questionnaire for Self-Assertiveness

Q1. Do you make an effort to do what you believe in, even if it means being unpopular with the people who love and care for you?

Q2. Do you live your life the way you want to?

Q3. Suppose you are forced to go to a party because of some obligation, do you think how you spend the time there is entirely in your control?

Q4. Do you ask for help when you know you need it?

Self-Assessment Questionnaire for Purposeful Living

Q1. Where do you see your career five years from now? Do you see growth? What kind of growth?

Q2. Do you have different sets of goals for different aspects of your life? Are they all time-bound, measurable, and achievable?

Q3. How do you keep track of progress for your different goals?

Q4. What are the elements that hinder your progress and what are those that facilitate your progress towards your goals?

Self-Assessment Questionnaire for Personal Integrity

Q1. How often do you lie to people, both in your personal and professional life? Why do you choose to lie?

Q2. Suppose you realize you have made a mistake at your office. You have an easy way to get away without being caught.

However, someone else ends up taking the blame. What will you do?

Q3. Are you leading a life that is perfectly aligned with your values and principles? If it is perfect, what and where are the deviations?

Chapter 3: Habits and How to Use Them for Good

Human beings are creatures of habits, and we don't know how to live without them. Reflect on a typical day at home, and you will see that nearly 90% of what you do is habitual in nature. We are unwittingly replacing old habits with new ones regularly. Habits can typically be divided into:

1. Indiscernible habits, such as tying shoelaces, bathing, brushing your teeth, etc.
2. Bad habits, such as overeating, smoking, putting off work, addictions, etc.
3. Good habits, such as daily exercise, eating nutritiously, getting a good night's rest each day, etc.

Everyone wants to build good habits and eliminate bad habits in their life. One way of doing this is to look at each bad habit, find its trigger, and work at it individually to break it or convert it into a good habit. For example, you can look at the bad habit of smoking and understand how it works in your body and mind, and break it slowly and steadily, or replace it with, perhaps, chewing gum, which is less harmful than smoking. Each habit needs to be handled differently and calls for different techniques to break (the bad ones) and build (the good ones).

In an attempt to bring all kinds of habits under one umbrella, Charles Duhigg, supported by years of research and surveys, came out with a book called, *'The Power of Habit,'* in which he discusses the habit loop in detail. You can take any habit of yours and fit it into this habit loop. Understanding the habit loop will enlighten you on how habit work. Once you comprehend this concept, then you can attack any bad habit and convert it into a good one, or simply eliminate it from your life.

The habit loop, as per Charles Duhigg, consists of:
- The Cue
- The Routine
- The Reward

The Cue

Also referred to as the trigger, this element puts your brain into the habit mode and compels it to perform the habit action (or the Routine). Cues can be of different types. Let us look at some of them:

Time cue – This is the most common form of cues for setting the habit routine in motion. For example, at around noon, you automatically reach out for your lunch. At around 3pm, you habitually step out for a coffee. Let us use this cue to understand the trigger of a bad habit.

Suppose you are to step out after lunch to meet your buddies at the cigarette shop for a smoke. This is at around 12.15 after lunch. From today, be conscious of your feelings at 12.15 after your lunch. What are your feelings? The urge for a cigarette?

The desire to be with your friends? Boredom or loneliness because there is nothing to do or nobody to talk to after having your lunch until your break time is over?

Study this cue in detail. Suppose it was an urge for a cigarette. Understand your emotions layer by layer. Is there physical pain if you don't have your cigarette? If yes, then it is possible that you need professional help to get out of this habit. However, if there is no physical pain, then analyze your urge for the cigarette. Can it be replaced with chewing gum? Or a cup of coffee? Or something else harmful? Can you move your lunchtime to 1pm instead of 12 noon? Will that make a difference to break the habit.

If the time cue drives the urge to be with friends, then can you find another place to meet them instead of the cigarette shop? If you are bored or lonely, can you identify someone in your office with whom you can share your lunch? Or can you carry a novel or book you can read during that time?

The primary lesson is that, by studying the time cue, you are consciously trying to understand how and what is driving you to the bad habit. When you know that element, you can find ways to break it or replace it with something that can start off a good habit instead of a bad one.

Location cue – Many times, being at a particular place sets off the bad habit. In the smoking example, the cigarette shop could be the trigger to buy yourself a cigarette and start smoking. So, to change that, change the location of the post-lunch meeting with your friends. Try a juice bar or a café that does not sell cigarettes. Alternately, carry a small pack of chewing gum (make sure it is the sugar-free ones) with you, and pick one from the pack instead of buying a cigarette.

Preceding events cue – What happens when your phone rings? You answer the call, and when it is over, you automatically scan through your notifications, right? That is a classic example of a preceding event cue. When you get the call, your brain is habituated into checking for notifications.

Now, on a busy day at your office, this habit can eat into a lot of time reducing your productivity and efficiency considerably. You must be conscious of it and battle it out with your brain not to scan notifications after answering the call. Alternately, keep notifications off while you are working. Then, there will be nothing to see.

You can use the preceding event cue to set up good habits. For example, your morning coffee is almost a done thing. Now, set up a habit of meditating for a couple of minutes after you finish your coffee. Another example would be before retiring to bed, use the sleeping time as a cue to make entries in your daily journal or create your to-do list for the next day.

Emotional status cue – Have you gone out drinking whenever something bad happened at your workplace? Do you reach for the bottle in the evening when your boss has criticized you? Your emotional status is one of the most common cues to trigger bad habits.

Emotions are always more difficult to overcome than time, location, and preceding events cues. Emotions can become so powerful that they tend to overwhelm us and the ability to act rationally reduces considerably. One of the most effective methods to manage emotions is to engage in some form of mood-enhancing activity, such as hitting the gym or going for a run. Use a punching bag to transfer your anger and sadness.

Another way to cope with overwhelming emotions is to practice mindfulness. By being mindfully aware of your emotions, you are allowing your body to feel the rush of anger or sadness and helping yourself from reacting in a regrettable way. Learn some basic and simple breathing exercises that facilitate a mindful state.

The company you keep – For example, if you spend every Friday evening with people who enjoy drinking, you are also going to be drinking. Avoid going out with this set of friends, at least on Friday evening when you know a booze session is bound to start with them.

Similarly, if you are having lunch with someone who eats excessively, you will also be driven to overeat. So, if you are trying to break the habit of overeating, avoid friends who tend to eat more than you should. Stick with people who consume sparse meals.

Surround yourself with people who keep good habits if you want to build good habits. And stay away from people who indulge in bad habits, and your resolve to get rid of them will become stronger than before.

The Routine

The routine in a habit loop is the actual action performed. For example, when you take that post-lunch break with your friends to smoke, the act of smoking itself is the routine. Looking up social media notifications after you complete your phone call is an example of the routine. Here are some ways you can alter the routines so that bad habits can become good habits:

- Replace the cigarette with fruit
- Replace the cigarette with your favorite book
- Use preceding events to remind you of good habit routines
- Meditate during emotional stress

The Reward

The reward is the final prize or the end-result of the habit loop. The brain decides the value of the habit based on the quality of the reward. For example, the joy of drinking is the reward for habitual drinkers. The brains of drinkers are habituated into storing, keeping track of, and recalling cues that trigger drinking because the joy of drinking is worthy of the effort.

Other rewards discussed in this chapter include:

- The thrill of reading useless but exciting gossip on social media

- The joy of overeating
- The joy of spending time with friends
- The calming (though temporary) effect of the alcohol

Changing bad habits to good ones can happen if you experiment with rewards. For example, you can try to meditate for a couple of minutes every time you complete a phone call. The stress-busting joy of even these short-duration meditations can give you the same but more productive joy of reading useless but exciting gossip on social media.

Make sure you have fruit handy wherever you so that you can overeat them to your heart's content, doing far less harm than overeating pizzas and burgers. The joy of spending time with friends can hardly be replaced. However, you can get the same joy if you can change the venue of your meeting place. How about meeting at the local gym and spending quality time with friends, even as you burn some calories in the process.

The calming effect of alcohol can easily be replaced by more sustainable rewards such as the peace of meditation, the stress-busting techniques associated with mindfulness living, or simply charging up your pheromones by hitting the gym or going for a run in the neighborhood park.

Therefore, follow the habit loop for all your habits, and make suitable changes at any or all of the three places (cue, routine, or reward) and replace your bad habits with good ones and enhance the quality of your life. With improved quality of life comes improved self-esteem driven by the results of doing things the right way.

Self-Discovery of Bad Habits

Here is a small (definitely not exhaustive) list of bad habits that men frequently get trapped by. Look at each of them and see if you are already in the throes or carry the risk of becoming addicted to that bad habit.

- Excessive eating and/or drinking
- Procrastinating
- Being late for an appointment or meeting
- Picking your nose or teeth in public
- Overuse of bad words
- Checking your mobile device in the middle of dinner
- Eating sloppily or with your mouth open
- Never pick up the tab when eating out with friends
- Snapping or popping gum in public
- Talking (even whispering) during a movie
- Not helping in the kitchen
- Addiction to social media, video games, YouTube videos
- Binge-watching TV serials or movies

Avoid putting off catching these and other bad habits and throwing them out of your life. The longer you put off this critical activity, the more difficult it will become because the habit is getting increasingly ingrained into your psyche with each passing day.

Step-by-Step Guide to Eliminate Bad Habits or Replace them with Good Ones

Step 1 - Identify one bad habit you intend to break. Start with the easiest one because the success of this will motivate you to try a harder next time. What are the cues for it? Who are the people around you at that time? What time does this cue typically get triggered? What are your emotions at that time?

Step 2 – What is the reward or craving that you find irresistible? Try other rewards that can result in the same satisfaction without the associated habit-forming negative side-effects. Experimenting with rewards should be an ongoing process. Keep trying until you have quit the bad habit.

Step 3 – Now, define the new routine with the new rewards. Put the new habit loop in place. Additionally, you must put up reminders and sticky-notes in obvious places until your brain becomes accustomed to the new habit.

Here is an example of setting a new habit: Before going to bed (the preceding event cue), I will make the to-do list (routine) for the next day. The result of being prepared and organized is the reward.

Here is an example of replacing old bad habits with new good ones: For my post-lunch (time cue) meet with my friends (the routine and reward), I will change the venue from the cigarette shop (old location) to the nearby park (new location) for a short game of baseball.

Alain De Botton, the renowned British philosopher, coach, and counselor, says, *"The best cure for your bad habits is to see it in action in another person."* Don't ever underestimate the debilitating harm an unresolved bad habit can cause. Work at it and root it out of your system.

Chapter 4: Practical Examples

This chapter gives you some practical examples of how you can work on the six components discussed in Chapter 2 to build and develop your self-esteem.

The Practice of Living Consciously

NLP Techniques

Neuro-Linguistic Programming (NLP) is a technique that is designed to align your conscious mind with your subconscious and unconscious mind. NLP techniques are proven to help in improving mindset, memory, intelligence, and communication skills. Here are some NLP techniques to help you lead a more conscious life:

Pay close attention to your thoughts – Our subconscious and unconscious minds are affected deeply by our thoughts. For example, if you have a presentation on Monday morning, and your thoughts are, "I know I'm going to a bad job," or "I think I am going to goof up big time on Monday," then your subconscious mind will send subtle signs to your body and conscious mind to resist your efforts to prepare well for the presentation.

On the contrary, if your thoughts are, "I'm sure I will be a hit with my presentation. I know I have taken care of all the details needed to make it a perfect piece," then your subconscious mind will tell your gross mind and body to work hard and ensure the presentation comes out perfectly on the D-day.

Don't forget to pray – Prayers to a supernatural being whom you believe is more endowed and more capable than you are nothing but hopes and self-wishes for good things to happen. Prayers render a strong sense of faith which drives you to work hard to achieve your wish.

For example, if you want that bonus really hard this year, then you pray every day to get it. Your conscious mind accepts the prayers and passes it on to the subconscious mind which will drive you to accept the importance and criticality of this prayer. The faith that spreads through your entire being will drive you to work hard to realize your dreams.

Affirmations – Affirmations are like mantras. The more you repeat, the deeper it gets ingrained into your psyche, which creates a positive aura around you leaving you powerful and strong to get what you want. Some examples of every day positive affirmations for living consciously:

- I accept responsibility for my life
- I am a wise, intelligent, and conscious human being
- I live a disciplined and balanced life
- I don't need other people's approval to be happy
- I do all my tasks with my heart, body, and soul
- I accept what I can control and also what I cannot control

- I have limitless potential and I can expand and grow to the best of my abilities

Visualization techniques – Visualization and imagination help you stay on the path of your goal without being negatively affected by external factors. There are multiple benefits of visualization or the happy moment or joy of achieving your dream. One of the primary benefits of visualization is that it helps you reach your maximum potential.

For example, if you can visualize running a 10K marathon, you might not suddenly become physically powerful to run a record time the next day. However, your subconscious mind will be driven to accept the reality of your imagination, and in turn, compel you to reach your maximum potential.

So, if you have an important presentation to give, visualize the success of your efforts and everyone lauding your work. It will help strengthen your resolve and motivation to really do well.

Meditation – Meditation is one of the most effective tools for living consciously. Meditation helps you connect with your deepest thoughts and emotions. In such a circumstance, you will be able to discern between the various emotions and understand the true nature of your thoughts.

Meditation helps you to remain in the moment so that your heart, mind, and soul are all synchronized together to give you a fabulously resonating experience in every single moment of your life.

Maintaining a diary – Making entries in your diary every day enhances your ability to live more consciously than before. Write down three positive and negative experiences of each day. Include the following details for each event:

- Details of the event
- Who were the other people present?
- When did it happen?
- What were your feelings?
- What were the lessons learned?

Many times, we get so emotionally caught up in a life experience that we cannot truly differentiate between the various emotions at that point. However, later on, when you are trying to record the event when it is fresh in the mind, you will find it easier to discern the different emotions that you felt.

For example, if your presentation went well, you would have felt a general sense of happiness. But, when you make an effort to write down the feelings, you will be able to recall other emotions and thoughts such as pride, relief, increased self-confidence, the resolve to take on more challenges in the future, and more. Additionally, you will be able to treat your negative experiences objectively, allowing you to take as many lessons as you can from them.

Therefore, maintaining a diary with daily entries will help you relive your experiences more consciously than before.

The Practice of Self-Acceptance

NLP Techniques

Anchoring technique – This NLP technique helps you anchor your positive experiences using physical sensations. Recall one of the most favorite and happiest moments of your life. Now, as you recall those positive emotions, touch the tip of your forefinger to the tip of your thumb. By doing this, you are anchoring that happy experience to this particular gesture. Whenever you are going through a phase of self-doubt, touch the tip of your forefinger to the tip of your thumb, and recall that joyful time again, and watch your self-doubt disappear. With repeated practice of this anchoring technique, you will notice that every time you bring the tips of your forefinger and thumb together, automatically your thoughts will go to that joyful experience. It's a perfect technique to shake off any feelings of self-doubt and biased criticism quickly.

Affirmations – Use the following affirmations for self-acceptance. Repeat them as often as you can, and definitely when you wake up in the morning to start off your day on a positive note.

- I deserve happiness, joy, and love
- I unconditionally accept and love myself the way I am
- I am complete on my own and do not need any external factors to make me feel whole.

- I will use this gift of life exuberantly and confidently

Visualization Techniques

Imagine yourself as happy and joyful at all times. Imagine you are always smiling irrespective of external circumstances. When you visualize a happy scene, your subconscious mind will accept it to be the truth and compel your gross body and conscious mind to work towards converting that visual image into reality.

When you love and accept yourself visually, it will be reflected in your body language as well. There will be a spring in your step, a smile on your face, and a positive aura around you. People naturally gravitate towards happy people. Therefore, your positivity will attract more people to you helping you build your level of self-confidence and self-esteem.

Meditation

Use the self-acceptance affirmations given above to meditate and increase the feel-good emotion in your life. When you are going through an emotionally tumultuous time, and you are unsure of yourself, find a quiet place where you will not be disturbed for about 5-10 minutes, close your eyes, and focus on your breath even as you repeat a suitable affirmation.

For example, if you are nervous before a presentation, and a nasty colleague passes a rude comment hoping to stifle your confidence, don't give in to the negative emotions flooding your body. Smile at your colleague, go out of the office, find a peaceful place to meditate and repeat the affirmation, "I am a confident person, and I approve of myself. I do not get discouraged by external factors." When the emotions have drained from your system, you will find yourself feeling noticeably more confident and not feeling bitter against your colleague. Self-acceptance makes you increasingly compassionate towards others.

Maintaining a Diary

Write down the talents and skills that you are proud of and the weaknesses you want to work on. Answer the following questions about yourself which will help you increase self-acceptance:

- Do I want the best for myself? Will I ever cheat myself? What should I do to trust myself more?
- What are the good things happening in my life that I know for certain I deserve? Why do I believe I deserve these good things?
- Suppose you did not get that promotion you were hoping to get last month. Were you disappointed? Why? Now, after a month, can you think of at least one good reason why you believe not getting that promotion was actually a good thing?

The Practice of Self-Responsibility

NLP Techniques

The NLP Swish technique – The Swish technique helps you replace a negative thought with a positive one so that your brain uses the same trigger to think positively. The Swish technique has the following elements:

- Unwanted thoughts and triggers
- Unwanted feelings
- Replacement thought

Let us take an example in your professional life where you can successfully use this NLP technique. Suppose you appeared for a promotion interview last year, and you were not selected for promotion. The same opportunity has come up again, and you want to go for the interview again. You have performed exceedingly well the last year, and your boss is pleased with you. You have brushed up your technical knowledge too and have updated yourself with the latest skills required for the new role you are applying for.

Yet, you are filled with apprehension driven by last year's failure. So, how can you replace the negativity with positivity using the Swish technique? Here's is what you should do:

Unwanted thoughts – are those that trigger a negative feeling in you. The thoughts could be visions of you failing again this year.

Unwanted feelings – are those emotions of fear and uncertainty

Replacement thoughts – You have undergone multiple mock interviews with your boss and your peers. You have done exceedingly well in many of them. Take an example of one such successful mock interview (preferably done with your boss) in which he or she has praised you for your efforts and said positive things about the potential outcome of the real interview.

Replace the unwanted thoughts with this positive and happy memory and relive that experience until the unwanted feelings are eliminated from your heart and mind. Use the NLP Swish technique to get rid of baseless self-doubts and fears and be prepared to face challenges with confidence.

Affirmations

Take responsibility for building and developing self-esteem, because no one else can really do it for you. Use any of the following affirmations to increase self-acceptance:

- I am totally responsible for my self-esteem and I will give my 100% to build it
- I am responsible for whatever is happening in my life
- I take responsibility for all my actions, behaviors, words, and everything I do or say
- I am not responsible for how others behave with me

Visualization Techniques

Visualization is a very strong tool to build your future in your mind which is then transmitted by the subconscious mind to your entire being driving you to give your best to make that visualization a reality. Here is an example of a visualization for self-acceptance:

- Sit comfortably in a quiet, undisturbed place.
- Close your eyes and imagine yourself entering your office elevator with confidence
- Visualize a happy smile on your face and a well-groomed profile.
- Imagine getting into the elevator and being greeted by colleagues and subordinates
- Visualize yourself responding with equal gusto
- Next, visualize yourself getting off from the elevator and crossing the long corridor to your cabin, nodding and greeting people on the way
- Next, visualize passing your boss' cabin, and peeping in to wish him or her good morning and receiving a positive greeting in return.
- Imagine a spring in your step as you get into your cabin and switch on the computer to get started for the day

A positive visualization such as this will help you get off to a great start.

Meditation

Look at this illustration. You have joined a local gym, and you have taken on the services of a dedicated trainer to help you with your fitness. Now, one day, you are lifting weights, and your trainer tells you to start with something heavier than the previous time. You are a bit hesitant, but your trainer tells you that if you are cautious, then it will be alright. So, you go ahead and listen to him.

Unfortunately, you pull a muscle while lifting the heavier weights as recommended by your trainer. You could, of course, blame your trainer for suggesting the idea. However, instead of reacting rashly, sit and meditate and focus your thoughts on the entire episode, and the following glaring ideas will come to the fore:

- Your lack of conviction in letting your trainer know that you are not ready for heavier weights
- Your loss of concentration when you pulled the muscles
- Acting with undue bravado
- Ignoring the pain that an initial couple of lifts gave you thinking it was normal

Meditating and focusing on the episode opened new vistas, giving you the required leeway to handle yourself in a calm, cool, and mature manner. This kind of attitude enhances your popularity, resulting in increased self-esteem.

Maintaining a Diary

Every day, make a note of two experiences that you did not like. Next to each one of them, write down at least two things you could have done to reduce the negative impact of the experience. As you practice this exercise, you will find it increasingly easy to take onus for all that is happening to you.

The Practice of Self-Assertiveness

NLP Techniques

One of the primary and most effective ways of asserting yourself is learning to say no. Look back at your professional life and list the number of times you should have ideally said no to your co-worker or boss or subordinate. Instead, you said yes, and have been trapped in your own cage, unable to wriggle out of problems.

Next time that bossy subordinate asks for leave, firmly say no to her. Get it right once, and you will be surprised how easy it is to a much more productive and efficient level of work than before. NLP techniques include deconstructing and formulating various scenarios in which you will practice mentally to say no so that when the real thing happens, your mind is ready for the challenge.

Affirmations

Some self-assertive affirmations for you:
- I am fearless and speak my mind
- I am a self-assertive man
- I can easily articulate my opinions and feelings to people
- I am a confident person
- I stand firm when the situation calls for it.

Visualization Techniques

Let us take the example of having to say no to your bossy subordinate next time she asks for leave with a valid reason. Here are some steps to help you visualize the scene:
- Imagine the lady walking into your cabin and asking for leave
- Visualize yourself making eye contact with her and looking confidently at her
- Imagine her discomfiture at this new attitude of yours
- Visualize yourself asking her for a valid reason for her leave request
- Imagine her struggling to come up with something
- Visualize yourself giving her an alternative that she simply cannot refuse

- Visualize her leaving your cabin humbly accepting defeat

Repeat this visualization in your mind until the fears of standing up and saying no disappear completely.

Meditation

Meditation is the perfect solution for self-assertiveness because it empowers you to see various perspectives of the same situation using which you can come up with multiple options to overcome nearly all challenges in your life effectively. Meditation teaches you to differentiate between assertiveness and aggression, thereby giving you the power to assert yourself without hurting other people.

Meditation enhances your self-awareness which, in turn, helps you articulate your needs unhesitatingly. Make meditation a daily habit. Spend about 15 minutes with yourself, learning to be comfortable in your own company. There are many occasions that you can find during the day to meditate. You could use your daily commute time to meditate, you could use your post-lunch walk, you could spend 15 minutes before retiring to bed, or any other convenient time.

Maintaining a Diary

In your diary, make a note of all the challenges you faced that day. Next to each challenge, write down affirmation statements to build your self-assertiveness and prepare yourself, should the occasion arise again. For example, your wife and you had a bitter battle after you returned from work in which she, perhaps, accused you of some untrue things, leaving you humiliated and insulted in front of your children. Without getting into her side of the story, use the following diary entry to recover from that difficult situation:

First, write down all the emotions you felt during the tiff: anger, sadness, resentment, and whatever else. Then, write down the following affirmation a couple of times next to this entry: Lies said in the rudest way or in the loudest voice do not become true. People who lie are only undermining themselves.

The Practice of Living Purposefully

NLP Techniques

Set SMART goals (a powerful and highly beneficial NLP tool) to live your life with purpose. Your goals should be:

S – Specific and not general: for example, 'I will complete the write-up of five of the ten cases allocated to me by the end of this week,' is a valid specific goal for a young lawyer. However, 'I will try to complete as many cases as I can by the end of this week' is not specific.

M – Measurable: for example, in the above case, each time one case write-up is done, the young lawyer can knock it off from his list and measure how many more he has left to complete the goal of 5 per week.

A – Achievable: for example, the young lawyer wanting to become a Supreme Court judge within weeks of getting his law certificate is not achievable

R – Realistic: for example, if the young lawyer had been allocated 50 cases, setting a goal of completing all the 50 within a week seems unrealistic.

T – Timebound: Goals must have a date beyond which they expire if you have failed to achieve them; for example, if the young lawyer had not put '5 cases by the end of this week,' it would is not timebound.

Affirmations

Affirmations for living purposefully:
- I am connected with my life purpose
- I know exactly what I want to achieve
- My inner voice keeps directing me to stay on my chosen path
- I live a passionate and purposeful life
- I dream big and work very hard to realize those big dreams

Visualization Techniques

Use the following visualization scenes to inch closer to your set goals:

- Visualize getting a promotion and being congratulated by your super-boss
- Visualize getting your boss' cabin allocated to you on promotion
- Visualize a nice increase in your pay
- Visualize a beautiful home by the beach in which you are living happily with your wife and kids
- Visualize going off on an exotic holiday with your family
- Visualize a lovely Thanksgiving dinner at home, surrounded by your loved ones who are looking at you with love and respect

Meditation

Living with a purpose has multiple challenges, and one of the biggest ones is to lose track of your purpose. Meditation is a great way to repeatedly remind yourself of your life goals. Spend a few minutes each day focusing on your purpose and your daily goals.

Maintaining a Diary

It is best to record your SMART goals divided into daily, weekly, and monthly targets into your diary. Record your progressions and hindrances along with solutions that worked for the challenges. You will never lose sight of your ultimate life goal.

The Practice of Personal Integrity

NLP Techniques

Personal integrity is all about showing your true character to the outside world. Here are some NLP-approved techniques to help you practice personal integrity:

- Learn to say NO because it will help you make only those promises that you are certain of delivering
- Learn self-discipline and focus so that you work efficiently and productively doing things that are aligned with your values and not wasting resources that are not aligned with your principles

Affirmations

Some affirmations for personal integrity:
- I promise to be honest and straightforward always
- I will promise only what I can deliver

- I take pride in owning up to my mistakes
- I will stand by my principles even if it means becoming unpopular

Visualization Techniques

Here are some visualization techniques to help build personal integrity:

- Imagine the happy faces of your loved ones when you keep your promises made to them
- Imagine the sad faces of your children when you say that the weekend picnic is going to be canceled because you need to work over the weekend
- Visualize the joy of your team members when you kept the promise of fighting to get them all a good raise for a job well done

Meditation

Meditation is the best way to get to know ourselves at the deepest level. This increased self-awareness helps us stay committed to our values and principles. Meditate regularly and understand yourself better.

Maintaining a Diary

In your diary, keep a list of broken promises to remind yourself of the pain you caused to the person concerned.

When a similar situation arises in which you run the risk of breaking another promise, retrieve your diary and use the entry made in it, especially about the pain in the face of the concerned individual. This will help you work hard and stand by your promise.

Chapter 5: Workbook

The workbook is based on the six components of self-esteem propounded by Nathaniel Branden in his book, 'The Six Pillars of Self-Esteem.' Complete the quizzes and questionnaires given at the end of the various chapters, specifically in Chapter 4. The answers to these questions and quizzes will give you your current status regarding the six components of self-esteem including:

- The practice of living consciously
- The practice of self-acceptance
- The practice of self-responsibility
- The practice of self-assertiveness
- The practice of living purposefully
- The practice of personal integrity

Based on your answers, rank the order of your current status of the six components started from your strongest point and move towards your weakest point. For example, suppose you got the best scores for living consciously and the worst scores for living purposefully. Do this workbook in reverse order. Basically, stand with that component which needs your immediate attention because you are lagging behind on it. Let us dive straight into the workbook now:

Workbook for the Practice of Living Consciously

NLP techniques – Pay Close Attention to Your Thoughts

Before going to bed, make a note of the three most enervating thoughts that was in your mind constantly today

1) _____
2) _____
3) _____

NLP techniques – Prayers

Every Sunday morning (best time is after you return from church; however, if you don't have a practice of going to church, then before you sit down for your breakfast), make a note of the three most crucial prayers that you definitely want answered during the week:

1)
_____
2)
_____
3)
_____

Affirmations – From the examples given in Chapter 4, or after researching on your own, make a note of the three affirmations that are best aligned with your choice to live consciously:

1) _____

___

2) _____

___

3) _____

___

Visualization – Visualize the most important purpose in your life and make detailed notes of the imagined scene. Remember to include:

The scene

_____

The people in it

_____

Smells

_____

Sounds

_____

Your feelings

_____

Meditation – Many times, despite our best efforts, some thoughts continue to haunt us right through the meditation session. After your meditation session, make a note of two of the topmost thoughts that refused to leave your mind:

1)

_____

—

2)

_____

—

Maintaining a diary – At the end of every week, read your journal entries. Identify at least one item that repeated twice (at a minimum) for which you had to be grateful. Don't stop at one if there are more. Write down all such items:

1)

_____

—

Workbook for the Practice of Self-Acceptance

NLP anchoring technique - Take two of the most beautiful memories of your life. Use the NLP anchoring technique to create happiness anchors so that you are prepared to use them during an emergency:

1)

_____

2)

_____

Affirmations – Create three affirmations for self-acceptance on your own without referring to the examples given in this book.

1) _____

—

2) _____

—

3) _____

—

Visualization – Write detailed notes of a situation when you were at your happiest. What happened? And what were the emotions? Who was responsible for giving you this level of happiness?

_____

Meditation – Meditate on any of the following affirmations that you created for yourself for the self-acceptance component:

1) _____
2) _____

Workbook for the Practice of Self-Responsibility

The NLP Swish technique – Make a note of three unwanted thoughts that trigger unwanted feelings. Next to each of these unwanted thoughts, write a replacement thought:

1) Unwanted trigger

_____

1) Replacement trigger

_____

2) Unwanted trigger

_____

2) Replacement trigger

_____

3) Unwanted trigger

_____

3) Replacement trigger

_____

Affirmation – Create two your own self-responsibility affirmations?

1) _____
_____

2) _____
_____

Visualization – What is the most important goal in your life? Visualize the day you will reach this goal. Make detailed notes of your visualization including scenes, smells, the joy of your loved ones, your own emotions, and everything else.

_____
_____

Meditation – Recall a painful experience in your life. Relive the experience and think about it without the associated emotions that were there in the original. Now, make a list of all factors that contributed to the pain. Categorize the factors under two separate headings:

Under your control

_____

—

Not under your control

_____

—

You can use your journal entries to identify such painful experiences.

Workbook for the Practice of Self-Assertiveness

NLP techniques – Look at the following examples and answer honestly:

If you had to choose between being with your family and having to go to an office party, which would you choose and why?

If you had to choose between a friend who never drinks and can be a very boring company and a friend who throws amazing parties, but you are sure to drink right through the night and come with a horrible hangover to work on most working days, who will you choose as your best friend?

Write down and visualize making the right choice in your mind so that when you encounter a similar real-life situation, your body and mind are prepared to choose appropriately and is duly backed by powerful reasons

Affirmations – Complete the following affirmations in your own words:

1) I am _____

2) I am undeterred by _____

3) I stand up for _____

Visualization – Remember that office situation when you had to say no to the bossy subordinate. You visualized it multiple times before you become perfect. Now, make detailed notes of that visualization and include all the elements: the words you chose, body language, gestures, tone of voice, etc.

Workbook for the Practice of Living with Purpose

NLP techniques – Make detailed notes of at least five important goals of your life making sure they fulfill the SMART goal-setting requirement:

S – Specific

M – Measurable

A – Achievable

R – Realistic

T – Timebound

Affirmations – Create your own three affirmations that are most suited to your life goals and purposes:

1) _____

2) _____

3) _____

Visualization – Rate the following goals in decreasing order of importance in your life:

Having a great career

Having a happy and peaceful family life

Being extremely wealthy

Traveling the world

Pursuing your music hobby

Now, visualize success for the top three goals, and make detailed notes of that success scene. Don't worry if none of the above goals are on your list. Simply make your own goal list, rate them, and write success stories of the top three goals.

Workbook for the Practice of Personal Integrity

NLP techniques – Here are some classic examples of saying no politely. Rate them in order of your preference. Practice using them daily. And, don't forget or hesitate to use them in real-life situations so that you can make only those promises that you can be certain of keeping:

I am really grateful to you for thinking of me, but right now my plate is really full.

Not my cup tea, thank you so much.

I am not really into gaming, but thank you for asking

I really appreciate your keenness in giving me this task, but I am excessively busy for the next couple of weeks.

Affirmations – Create three of your own affirmations most suitable for your way of living:

1) _____
   _____

2) _____
   _____

3) _____
   _____

Maintaining a diary – Think of two of the most difficult experiences in your life when you broke a promise. Now, answer the following questions:

What were reasons for letting the concerned person down?
_____
—

How did you feel about it?
_____
—

What were the lessons learned from those experiences that helped improve your level of personal integrity?
_____

—

Conclusion

The journey of building and developing your self-esteem definitely has a starting point, and that is the moment you choose to take action. However, there is no end-point. It is a continuous and unending learning process. As your progress on your path, you only get better than your previous state. However, there will never come the point when you can say, "I have learned everything that has to be learned in the realm of self-esteem, and there is no more room for improvement."

You must endeavor continuously to grow and build on the six crucial components of self-esteem including:

1. Living consciously
2. Self-acceptance
3. Self-responsibility
4. Self-assertiveness
5. Living with purpose
6. Personal integrity

Additionally, this book needs to be reread a couple of times and the quizzes and questionnaires repeated each time you think your level of self-esteem has gone up a few notches. The most important element of this book is to increase self-awareness by completing the chapter-end self-assessment repeatedly.

Perhaps, the best way to end this book is with self-esteem quotes of famous and successful people. So, here goes:

Self-esteem is as important to human beings as legs are to a table. It is the foundation that supports our mental and physical happiness – Louise Hart, the hit musician from Denmark

There is overwhelming evidence that proves that the higher the level of self-esteem, the more the person will treat others respectfully, generously, and kindly – Nathaniel Branden

www.ingramcontent.com/pod-product-compliance
Lightning Source LLC
Chambersburg PA
CBHW052121110526
44592CB00013B/1705